Prayers That Will Change Your Life

Kerrick A. R. Butler II

Carol,
These prayers will really
change your life!

Kerrick Butler

CONTENTS

YOUR PRAYER LIFE MATTERS

Prayer changes things. We have heard this expression many times. In its simplest form, prayer is communication with God. Prayer connects the Believer to the unlimited power of God and makes it available for their everyday life. The importance and need for prayer is seen throughout the narrative of the Bible in both the Old and New Testament. Even throughout history, awakenings that have changed the course of human events have been rooted in individuals giving themselves to prayer.

There are many wonderful revelations on prayer. One of the most important ones, to me, is that there are many different types of prayer. Paul addresses that subject in his letter to the church at Ephesus. Ephesians 6:18 says, "And pray in the Spirit on all occasions with all kinds of prayers and requests…" (NIV)

There are different kinds or types of prayer found in the Word of God. There is the prayer of dedication and commitment. There are prayers of intercession and supplication. There is the prayer that concerns the confession of sins for forgiveness. There is the prayer of faith and praying in other tongues. There is prayer where "groaning" and travail are involved. All of these kinds of prayer are powerful and important. Some of these kinds of prayers can be initiated by Believers while others have to be initiated by the Holy Spirit in the life of the yielded praying Believer.

Every prayer should be based on the Word of God. The will of God is the Word of God. It is important to pray the will of God in prayer because we have the assurance that God hears us.

1 John 5:14-15 tells us, "And this is the confidence that we have in him, that, if we ask any thing according to his will, he heareth us: And if we know that he hear us, whatsoever we ask, we know that we have the petitions that we desired of him."

Prayers rooted in the Word of God can be prayed by quoting the Scriptures in prayer or making requests in prayer in line with the revealed will of God. Many Christians have the misguided belief that if it is the will of God, there is no reason to pray about it. 1st Timothy 2:1-4 contradicts that belief.

"I exhort therefore, that, first of all, supplications, prayers, intercessions, and giving of thanks, be made for all men; For kings,

and for all that are in authority; that we may lead a quiet and peaceable life in all godliness and honesty. For this is good and acceptable in the sight of God our Saviour; Who will have all men to be saved, and to come unto the knowledge of the truth." 1 Timothy 2:1-4

It is the will of God that all men will be saved; even though that is God's will, we are still instructed to pray for the lost and pray for laborers to be able to reach them. (Matthew 9:38) The will of God is not automatic. God has His part to play and we have our part to play. God will not force you to receive the wonderful benefits of prayer even though He has provided everything necessary for you to receive those benefits. You must play your part; your prayer life matters.

While prayer can be an extemporaneous expression from the heart, it can also be read from the Scripture, or written and then prayed. As long as prayer is rooted in the Word of God and prayed with faith in God, prayer, no matter the kind or form, is powerful.

The four prayers of *Prayers That Will Change Your Life* are found in the Pauline Epistles, the letters of the Bible written by Paul the Apostle. Each chapter will explain these prayers in detail so that your faith will be stronger in these prayers that the Holy Spirit has so graciously provided us. As you pray these prayers, you will grant access for the Holy Spirit to do a wonderful work in your life. Pray these four prayers everyday and your life will be gloriously changed.

- Kerrick

THE EPHESIANS 1 PRAYER

PRAYER FOR WISDOM AND REVELATION

The Ephesians 1 Prayer, as the name suggests, is taken from Ephesians 1:15-23. This Biblical prayer is the Apostle Paul's heart's desire for the church at Ephesus and for Believers everywhere. As the Holy Spirit saw fit to include this prayer in the Scriptures, it is His heart's desire as well that the Believer receive the benefits of this prayer which range from wisdom, insight, spiritual perception, and more.

"Wherefore I also, after I heard of your faith in the Lord Jesus, and love unto all the saints, Cease not to give thanks for you, making mention of you in my prayers; " Ephesians 1:15-16

The Apostle starts his prayer for the church at Ephesus by thanking God for them. Thanksgiving and praising God is important to the Believer's faith and prayer life. Paul beginning his prayer with praises echoes the truth of Psalm 100:4 which says, "Enter into his gates with thanksgiving, and into his courts with praise: be thankful unto him, and bless his name." Believers should start everyday and every time of prayer with gratitude to God for all the things He has done for them.

Paul continues by saying that he makes mention of the church in his prayers. As much as possible, when praying for individuals, call their name out before God in prayer. Sometimes in prayer, Believers need to pray for groups such as their churches, their neighborhoods, their local law enforcement, and other groups with a large number of people. In such instances, it may not be possible to call out everyone's name due to time or they may not know everyone's name. Even then, Believers can pray for those groups and their prayer can still be effective.

Spirit of Wisdom and Revelation

"That the God of our Lord Jesus Christ, the Father of glory, may give unto you the spirit of wisdom and revelation in the knowledge of him:" Ephesians 1:17

In verse 17, Paul begins his actual prayer by referring to God as "the God of our Lord Jesus Christ" and "the Father of Glory." These titles carry weight and reveal important truths. When the Scripture says, "the God of our Lord Jesus Christ" it should remind the reader of the submission and obedience of Jesus. Although Jesus was 100% God and 100% man, He was submitted to the will of His Heavenly Father. Philippians chapter 2 speaks of Jesus' obedience to the will of God.

"Let this mind be in you, which was also in Christ Jesus: Who, being in the form of God, thought it not robbery to be equal with God: But made himself of no reputation, and took upon him the form of a servant, and was made in the likeness of men: And being found in fashion as a man, he humbled himself, and became obedient unto death, even the death of the cross. Wherefore God also hath highly exalted him, and given him a name which is above every name: That at the name of Jesus every knee should bow, of things in heaven, and things in earth, and things under the earth; And that every tongue should confess that Jesus Christ is Lord, to the glory of God the Father."

Philippians 2:5-11

In order to receive the fullness of the blessing that this prayer provides, the Believer should make up their mind to follow the example of the obedience of Jesus. Sometimes people are nervous about the will of God because it is a mystery to them. Even if a Believer does not know the will of God, this prayer will help them discern it, they can trust the will of God. God is good and His will for every Believer is an extension of His goodness. To doubt that God's will for the Believer is good would be to doubt His character. He is good and He has good things planned for each and every person. It is a good life filled with the fulfillment they were created to experience. In praying this prayer, a Believer should settle in their heart that they will do whatever their Heavenly Father tells them to do just like Jesus.

Paul also referred to God as "the Father of Glory." When the Apostle calls Him "the Father of Glory," he is letting the reader know that the glory comes from God. He is the originator of the glory. The Hebrew word for glory paints the picture that the Glory of God is heavy with everything good. The Greek definition for God's glory includes His magnificence, splendor, honor, and abundance. What Paul is about to ask for in prayer is coming from the glory of God. The result and answer of this prayer is the glory of God manifesting in a very specific way.

From this wonderful glory comes "the spirit of wisdom and revelation in the knowledge of Him." Wisdom is defined as correctly applied knowledge. It is not simply knowledge. This is a generation where people are receiving information and knowledge at greater rates that any other time in human history. Although a person can receive massive amounts of knowledge and information, if they do not know how to apply it, it will not be beneficial to them.

Paul is praying that Believers would receive more than just the spirit of wisdom, but revelation as well. Revelation is defined as a disclosure; an enlightening. It is a revealing. Imagine a grand theater that has a royal purple curtain at the front of the stage. Behind this curtain, is a magnificent set that will help the actors portray the story that they are telling the audience. When the curtain is pulled back, the set is revealed. The set did not magically appear when the curtain was removed, it was simply revealed. Revelation works the same way.

This prayer is not concerning general wisdom or revelation, but wisdom and revelation in the knowledge of Him. Knowledge, as it is defined for this Scripture, is recognition, full discernment, and understanding. It is being fully able to grasp and comprehend what is obscure. The Amplified Classic Edition renders this part of the verse as "deep and intimate knowledge of Him." The Message version translates this part of the verse as "to make you intelligent and discerning in knowing Him personally."

This knowledge is not knowledge that is gained by only studying, but a knowledge that also comes from an intimate relationship of knowing someone personally. God wants Believers to know Him intimately. Stop and think about that. The Apostle is praying that the Believer will have full disclosure and be able to grasp and perceive the intimate knowing of God personally and will be able to correctly apply that knowledge. As a husband, I have spent so much time with my wife, I can pick out her voice in a crowd; I can tell by a look what she may be thinking; I have learned when to offer advice or when to simply listen. This is the type of "knowing" that God wants us to have with Him. The fact God desires to have this type of "knowing" with every Believer is a marvelous testament of God's kindness. The knowing and its accurate application can produce wonderful results in the life of the Believer.

This is the type of knowledge the Apostle Peter is referring to in 2nd Peter 1:2 when he says that grace and peace are multiplied to the Believer "through the knowledge of God and of Jesus our Lord." One of the tremendous results of this Ephesians 1 prayer is that the Believer would have grace and peace multiplied in their everyday life. Every Believer can benefit greatly from an overflowing amount of grace and peace!

The Ephesians prayer upgrades the Believer's spiritual perception and insight.

The Eyes of Your Understanding

"The eyes of your understanding being enlightened; that ye may know what is the hope of his calling, and what the riches of the glory of his inheritance in the saints,"

Ephesians 1:18

The Believer being granted the spirit of wisdom and

revelation in the knowledge of Him causes the eyes of their understanding to be enlightened. Eyes speaks to the Believer's vision and spiritual sight. In this Scripture, understanding is defined as the mind, deep thought, and imagination. The word, "enlightened" means to brighten up or to be illuminated. The Amplified Classic Edition uses the phrase "flooded with light." This Ephesians 1 prayer is a prayer which results are upgrading of the Believer's spiritual perception and insight.

The Good News Translation translates this portion of the verse as, "I ask that your minds may be opened to see His light." Every person's life is greatly effected by their perspectives and mentality. The incorrect mentality can keep a person trapped and robbed of their full potential. There are many things that can cause a person's vision to be dimmed, darkened, and even blinded: how they were raised, by fear, by incorrect teaching, by abuse, etc. An individual can also close their own eyes through unbelief and disobedience. Jesus speaks of individuals closing their own eyes in Matthew 13.

"And in them is fulfilled the prophecy of Esaias, which saith, By hearing ye shall hear, and shall not understand; and seeing ye shall see, and shall not perceive: For this people's heart is waxed gross, and [their] ears are dull of hearing, and **their eyes they have closed**; lest at any time they should see with their eyes, and *hear with their ears, and should understand with their heart, and should be converted, and I should heal them."*

Matthew 13:14-15

Notice in the bolded phrase, the individuals closed their own eyes. They made a decision to close their eyes. As a result, they could not understand with their heart or be healed. Closed eyes can prevent individuals from receiving God's best for them.

Satan understands the power of keeping all people, Believers and non-believers, in the dark. Paul reveals blinding of minds as one of Satan's method of operations in 2nd Corinthians 4:3-4:,

"But if our gospel be hid, it is hid to them that are lost: In whom the god of this world hath blinded the minds of them which believe not, lest the light of the glorious gospel of Christ, who is the image of God, should shine unto them."

The lost have had their minds and visions blinded by the Enemy. It is through darkness that he keeps people from seeing the light of the glorious gospel of Christ. In this passage, Satan is called the "god of this world." Notice the lower-case "g." Satan is by no means God, but he is the ruler of this world. When the New Testament writers use "world," in this sense they are not speaking of the earth but the systems of the world. Satan is the ruler of the systems of the world. This world's systems are designed by Satan to keep individuals in darkness and alienated from the promises of God.

When the Believer prays the Ephesians 1 prayer, it can effect the vision of those who have closed their own eyes or those who have been blinded by Satan and the systems of the world. Not only should a Believer pray this prayer for themselves daily, but they should also pray this prayer for backslidden and unsaved loved ones. The results of this prayer can cause light to shine in the eyes of those who are far from God so they can truly see Jesus and turn to Him.

Remember, this prayer is still important for Believers who have not closed their eyes or have their minds blinded by Satan. The Heavenly Father does not want His children's vision to be dimmed, but ever increasing in light. God wants the Believer's vision and mentality to be flooded with light so that they may know what is the hope of His calling.

In this Scripture, hope is confident expectation. Many Believers have heard and used phrases about being "called by God" or "God's calling." The calling of God is simply His invitation. When God calls a person to a specific task, He is inviting them to fulfill His will in that area. An invitation can be received or rejected. Every individual has a God-given right to either receive or reject God's invitation. There are some who miss God's invitation for His purpose for their lives, because they do not see it or recognize it. The Ephesians 1 prayer enables Believers to know the confident expectation of God's invitation for their lives. The will of God and His invitation does not have to be a mystery towards Believers. God wants every Believer to receive His invitation and have clarity concerning the call on their lives. With clarity, the Believer can know what God expects from them and develop their own confident expectation that they will fulfill the call of God on their lives.

Riches of the Glory

When the Scriptures refer to the "riches of the glory," it is referring to the abundance of the glory. Romans 8:17 reveals that every Believer in an heir of God and a joint heir with Jesus. Since Believers are heirs, God has left them a tremendous inheritance. God has placed in every Believer's spirit an abundance of glory. In this prayer, Paul is praying that every Believer would know what is the abundance of the glory of God's inheritance in the Saints.

If Paul has to pray this way, then it is very possible for someone to have the abundance of glory on the inside of them and never know it! Paul is desiring that the Believer would know what the inheritance is so that they can access it and benefit from it. The Hebrew word for "glory" in the Old Testament can be described as "heavy with everything good." There is an abidance of everything good inside the Believer because of their inheritance.

In Ephesians 1:13 and 14, the Scripture shares that the Holy Spirit is the downpayment of our inheritance. The downpayment, or earnest as the KJV translates it, is the first payment. When individuals buy a house, unless they are paying the full cost, they pay a down payment. A downpayment is an indicator that there will be future payments. The Holy Spirit is the Believer's downpayment indicating there will be more glory for them to experience in their lives and even more when they receive their eternal reward. Although the eternal reward is wonderful, this prayer is for Believers to know and live in the abundance of glory in their lifetime on this earth.

The Exceeding Greatness of His Power

"And what is the exceeding greatness of his power to us-ward who believe, according to the working of his mighty power, Which he wrought in Christ, when he raised him from the dead, and set him at

his own right hand in the heavenly places, Far above all principality, and power, and might, and dominion, and every name that is named, not only in this world, but also in that which is to come: And hath put all things under his feet, and gave him to be the head over all things to the church, Which is his body, the fulness of him that filleth all in all."

Ephesians 1:19-23

The next thing that Paul desires the Believers to understand is what is the exceeding greatness of God's power that is available for those who believe. Believers are not powerless! According to this prayer, every Believer has access to the greatest power of the universe. This power is the same power that God used when He raised Jesus from the dead and set Him far above anything and everything. When Paul prays "exceeding greatness," he is saying "far beyond greatness." Imagine the greatest display of power you can think of; the power of your favorite superhero; the Apostle is saying that this power is far beyond that! That magnificent power is not just for a few special people; God desires this power to be active in the life of every single Believer!

This power is supernatural and miraculous ability. It is miraculous force and dynamic power. The power is available, but it is according to the working of God's mighty power. The word working here implies efficiency. Although this miraculous force is mighty, many Believers do not see it manifest consistently or to any high degree of power. One of the reasons is because of a lack of efficiency in their spiritual life where the power is concerned. The next chapter will go into greater detail about how a Believer can have that power manifest efficiently and effectively.

Ephesians chapter 1 ends with a reminder to the Believer about the tremendous position God has given them. After stating that God, through His power, lifted Jesus higher than anything, Paul states that that Father has placed Jesus to be the head over all things to the Church. Paul continues and states that the Church is Jesus' body, the fullness of Him that fills all in all.

If the head is seated far above everything, then so is the body. Paul reiterates the position of the Church in Ephesians 2:6 when he says that Believers are seated at the right hand of God in Christ Jesus. God has placed everything under the feet of the Church and the Church is the fullness of Jesus that fills all in all.

When the Apostle says that the Church is the fullness of Jesus that fills all in all, he is explaining that through the Church the presence, actions, and words of Jesus can fill the entire earth. As the Believers' eyes are opened to this truth, they are enabled to take their place in filling their area of the world with the presence and power of Jesus.

Before continuing to the next chapter, take a few moments and pray this prayer for yourself:

Father,
I pray that you, the God of our Lord Jesus Christ, the Father of glory, may give me the spirit of wisdom and revelation in the knowledge of you. I pray that the eyes of my understanding are enlightened; that I may know what is the hope of your calling, and what are the riches of the glory of your inheritance in the saints, and what is the exceeding greatness of your power to us who believe, according to the working of your mighty power, which you wrought in Christ, when you raised Him from the dead, and set Him at your own right hand in the heavenly places, far above all principality, and power, and might, and dominion, and every name that is named, not only in this world, but also in that which is to come. You have put all things under His feet, and gave him to be the head over all things to the church, which is His body, the fullness of him that fills all in all. Father, I thank you that when you seated Jesus at your right hand you have also seated me. In Jesus' name I pray, Amen.

THE EPHESIANS 3 PRAYER

PRAYER FOR SPIRITUAL STRENGTH

As Paul continues his letter to the church at Ephesus, he includes another wonderful, Spirit inspired prayer. In the beginning of chapter 3, Paul describes the ministry God has entrusted him with and the pressure, or tribulation, he faces as a result of it. The Apostle does not want the church of Ephesus to be overwhelmed because of what he's facing, but be strengthened by the Spirit This desire leads him to pen the following prayer.

Strengthened by the Spirit

"Wherefore I desire that ye faint not at my tribulations for you, which is your glory. For this cause I bow my knees unto the Father of our Lord Jesus Christ, Of whom the whole family in heaven and earth is named, That he would grant you, according to the riches of his glory, to be strengthened with might by his Spirit in the inner man;"
Ephesians 3:13-16

The grant, that Paul is requesting, comes from the riches of God's glory. As previously explained, the riches of the glory is the abundance of the glory. Within the abundance of glory, there is supernatural might. This might, according to the context of this prayer, will keep the Believer from fainting, giving up, or being overwhelmed. The supernatural might is located within every Believer.

The Holy Spirit lives inside every single Believer and therefore supernatural might is available to everyone who has received Jesus as their Lord and Savior. Although this might is available, not everyone accesses it or uses it. As seen in Ephesians 3, one of the ways to access this might is through faith-filled prayer.

The Ephesians 3 Prayer grants the Believer access to the might of God which will enable them to face any pressure life, this world, or the enemy would try to throw their way. The might is released in "inner man." The "inner man" is the spirit of the human. Men and women are tri-part beings. Every human is a spirit, possesses a soul, and lives in a body. The soul is the mind, will, and *seat* of the emotions. Although the might will be accessed by prayer, the Believer must use it to benefit from it. In order to use the might, the Believer must say that he has this might, make decisions based on following the leading of God's Spirit, and head in that direction.

Christ Dwell in Hearts by Faithfulness

"That Christ may dwell in your hearts by faith; that ye, being rooted and grounded in love," Ephesians 3:17

The next request Paul makes in this prayer is "that Christ may dwell in your hearts by faith." The Born Again Believer already has Jesus living on the inside of them. The writings of Paul and John attest to that wonderful truth time and time again. Since that is the case, Paul is not praying that Jesus would move into the heart of the Believer. The word "Christ" is not Jesus' last name. Christ describes Who Jesus is. Christ means the Anointed One. When you refer to the Anointed One, you also refer to the anointing that He has.

Throughout the Pauline Epistles, Paul's usage of "Christ" can refer to Jesus, His anointing, or both Jesus and His anointing. What is the anointing and the anointing that is on Jesus?

The anointing is the Holy Spirit and His burden removing, yoke destroying power.

"And it shall come to pass in that day, that his burden shall be taken away from off thy shoulder, and his yoke from off thy neck, and the yoke shall be destroyed because of the anointing."
Isaiah 10:27

"How God anointed Jesus of Nazareth with the Holy Ghost and with power: who went about doing good, and healing all that were oppressed of the devil; for God was with him."
Acts 10:38

The Apostle does not want the church to give up, so he prays that the anointing would dwell in their hearts by faith. The phrase "by faith" gives a clue to how much anointing will be accessible and dwell in the Believer's heart. The anointing available is proportionate to the faith of the individual. Romans 12:3 says that every Believer has been given the same measure of faith. Faith has to be developed and increased. This is the reason why many Believers are at various levels of faith. Some develop their faith and some do not. Romans 10:17 states that faith comes by hearing and by hearing the Word of God. Faith comes by the continual hearing of God's Word. Faith is developed through the hearing of the Word, speaking the Word, doing the Word, and having a close relationship with Jesus, the Word made flesh. Anyone can develop their faith; always remember, developing faith is not an one day occurrence, but a lifestyle.

Be Rooted and Grounded in Love

"That Christ may dwell in your hearts by faith; that ye, being rooted and grounded in love, May be able to comprehend with all saints what is the breadth, and length, and depth, and height; And to know the love of Christ, which passeth knowledge, that ye might be filled with all the fulness of God."
Ephesians 3:17-19

The next request the Apostle makes is for the church to be rooted and grounded in love. If you are rooted and grounded in love, you are secured and established on that love. Paul desires that all Believers everywhere would be able to comprehend the amazing love of Jesus Christ. He passionately prays that they would know the width, length, depth, and height of that love; that love is greater than all knowledge and comprehension. God's love is bigger, wider, and deeper than the Grand Canyon. How can a person understand something that is so vast it is greater than all knowledge and comprehension? With the help of the Holy Spirit, the Believer who prays this prayer will grow in a deeper understanding of how much God loves them, all of humanity, and creation. The Apostle prays that the Believer might "know" this love. The word that Paul uses for "know" expresses that he wants Believers to have a revelation of this love in a personal, intimate, and practical way.

A greater understanding of this love would lead the Believer to live according to this love. There is a saying that "hurting people hurt people"; let's reverse this saying; " loving people love people". Knowing, understanding, and experiencing God's love will cause Believers to love others in a deeper, selfless way. Believers will live the Love

Commandment because God's love is overflowing in their lives. Living in this love would have the Believer live 1st Corinthians 13:4-8 on a continual basis. The revelation that Paul is praying for the Believer to grasp would lead to an entire lifestyle transformation. The "love walk" would increase to such a point the person would love just like Jesus and resemble Him in their every day actions.

One of the amazing benefits for Christians believing God's extravagant love towards them is what it does to their faith. Galatians 5:6 explains that faith works by love. In the same way that some cars are fueled by gas, faith is fueled by love. Faith that is fueled by love can access the anointing that has been made available in the heart of the Believer. This wonderful realization leads to Paul's next request, "that ye might be filled with all the fulness of God."

As previously shared, God dwells within the Believer. Yet, Paul prays that each Believer will be filled with the fullness of God. This statement informs that it is possible for a person to be filled with the fullness of God. Every Believer's goal should be to be filled with the fullness of God. Many Believers can be filled with God, but it does not mean they are filled with His fullness. As the Believer grows in spiritual maturity and their relationship with God, their capacity to receive expands. As their capacity expands, they can be filled with more of Him. As they walk with Him, they will realize things in their life that need to be removed and changed. As they remove those things, those areas of their life can be filled with God. To be filled with the fullness of God is a lifetime pursuit and is a life that is worth pursuing. Paul's prayer does not end in verse 19, but continues with verse 20 and 21.

According to the Power Working in Us

"Now unto him that is able to do exceeding abundantly above all that we ask or think, according to the power that worketh in us, Unto him be glory in the church by Christ Jesus throughout all ages, world without end. Amen." Ephesians 3:20-21

It is wonderful that God can do far beyond everything that Believers can ask, think, dream, and imagine. Believers often overlook this part of the verse: "according to the power that is working in them". The Believer can easily limit the power of God from working in their lives. The majority of Christians do it everyday without realizing it. They may not realize the power is available and never consider it. They may continually makes decisions that are in opposition to the power working in their everyday life. This prayer holds revelation on how to have that power working or active in the Believer's life. In summary, this passage reveals that it is through prayer, faith-fueled by the revelation and the lifestyle of love, accessing the power, and putting it into everyday use that the Believer can experience fullness, expansion, and more of the fullness of God. By continually doing these things, the power will be working and active in the Believer's life. As the Believer continues to do these things, they will begin to see more of this magnificent ability of God manifest in their life. If they continue, they will live in amazement of seeing God do far beyond everything they pray, think, dream, and imagine.

In the benediction of this prayer, Paul proclaims for there to be glory, praise, honor, and fame given to God through the church by Christ Jesus forever. It should be the

Christian's desire and prayer everyday and throughout eternity to bring honor, praise, fame, and glory to God.

Before continuing to the next chapter, take a few moments and pray this prayer for yourself:

Father,
I pray that you would grant me, according to the riches of Your glory, to be strengthened with might by your Spirit in the inner man. I pray that Christ may dwell in my heart by faith and that I am being rooted and grounded in love, and may be able to comprehend with all saints what is the breadth, and length, and depth, and height; and to know the love of Christ, which passeth knowledge, that I might be filled with all the fulness of God. Father, I thank you that you are able to do exceeding abundantly above all that I ask or think, according to the power that is at work in me. Unto You be glory in my life and the church by Christ Jesus forever. In Jesus' name, Amen.

THE PHILIPPIANS 1 PRAYER

PRAYER FOR LOVE OVERFLOWING

The Apostle Paul begins his letter to the church at Philippi with great gratitude for their partnership in helping him spread the Gospel. In verse four, Paul reveals that every time he prays for the Philippians church he prays with joy. In addition to joy and gratitude, the Apostle expresses his great confidence in the Philippian saints in verse six. Lastly before his prayer, Paul expresses how much he loves and misses all of the saints at Philippi.

Love Overflowing

"And this I pray, that your love may abound yet more and more in knowledge and in all judgment;"

Philippians 1:9 KJV

In praying from a place of great love, joy, gratitude, and confidence, the Apostle requests that their love may overflow more and more past any previous amount or limitation. Romans 5:5 teaches that the Holy Spirit has poured the love of God into every Believer's heart. If the love of God can overflow, it can also operate in in smaller quantities or larger quantities. The previous chapter showed how the Believer's faith works by love in the same way that some cars are fueled by gas. In this instance, the vehicle can only go as far as the amount of fuel in its tank. In the same way, some Believers' faith only goes so far because of the lack of love operating in their hearts and lives. The Believer should be rooted in the love of God and continually overflowing in that love. Paul prays that this love overflows in knowledge and in all judgment. In this Scripture, judgment is referring to perception and discernment.

When the love of God overflows in knowledge and judgment, its operating at a high level with exact knowledge, discernment, and perception. It has been widely discussed that different individuals receive love in different ways. When this love overflows as described in Philippians 1, it enables the Believer to love in the best way the situation calls for love to be shown. This is an overflowing love and ability that can manifest God's love to meet the need at hand with specificity.

"That ye may approve things that are excellent; that ye may be sincere and without offence till the day of Christ."

Philippians 1:10

The Apostle is praying that their love overflows in this way, so that the Philippian Believers may approve things that are excellent and that they may be sincere and without offense until the return of Jesus. In approving things that are excellent, the Believer is examining the things in their life that they may determine what is the best course of action. The highest course of action is always the way of love. According to 1st Corinthians, love is the "more excellent way." This prayer helps the Believer develop their decision making in order to align themselves up with the excellent way of love. This leads the Believer to a lifestyle that is pure, faultless, and not troubled by a consciousness of sin because it is following the commandment of love. This is the lifestyle that each and every Believer should strive to live until the return of Christ.

Live a More Excellent Way

"Being filled with the fruits of righteousness, which are by Jesus Christ, unto the glory and praise of God."

Philippians 1:11

The lifestyle of the "more excellent way" is maintained by the fruits of righteousness which are described in Galatians 5:22-23 as the fruit of the Spirit. These fruits are the character traits of Jesus that the Holy Spirit wants to bring to prominence in the life of every Believer. These fruits of right living are meant to fill the life of the Believer. The fruit of the Spirit come through Jesus Christ. The development of the fruits of righteousness can only come through the Believer's relationship with Jesus. The more the Believer spends time in His presence, reading His Word, and following Him the more the Holy Spirit can grow the fruit of the Spirit in the Believer. In the same way a person can spend significant amount of time with another and begin to act like them, as a Believer spends more time with Jesus they will begin to act like Him.

The "glory and the praise of God" is the result of the Believer overflowing in love; being enabled to love with specificity; examining and aligning their lives with the more excellent way of love; and being filled with the fruit of the Spirit. The lifestyle described in these few verses of Philippians causes others to honor God and give Him praise. The Message version pictures the result of this lifestyle beautifully. It says that this way of life makes, "Jesus Christ attractive to all, getting everyone involved in the glory and praise of God."

Before continuing to the next chapter, take a few moments and pray this prayer for yourself:

Father,

I pray, that in me your love may abound yet more and more in knowledge and in all judgment. I pray that I may approve things that are excellent and that I may be sincere and without offense util the day of Christ. I pray that I am being filled with the fruits of righteousness, which are by Jesus Christ, unto Your glory and praise. In Jesus' Name I pray, Amen.

THE COLOSSIANS 1 PRAYER

PRAYER FOR SPIRITUAL GROWTH

The Apostle Paul begins his letter to the church at Colosse addressing their spiritual growth. Paul is writing this letter in response to the wonderful things he has heard about the the Colossian church. In verse four, he writes concerning their faith and the love they have for all of those in the Body of Christ. In verse six, he comments that the Word of God that was preached to them has brought forth fruit in their lives. The Apostle then adds that Epaphras, a minister at the church in Colosse, brought a good report to him concerning the Spirit-inspired love that the church operates in. As a result of what Paul has heard and the report of Epaphras, Paul began praying for this church on a continual basis. Even though the church was excelling and succeeding, there was greater growth that Paul wanted them to experience.

Filled With the Knowledge of His Will

"For this cause we also, since the day we heard [it], do not cease to pray for you, and to desire that ye might be filled with the knowledge of his will in all wisdom and spiritual understanding;"

Col 1:9

Paul begins his praying that the Believers would be "filled with the knowledge of His will in all wisdom and all spiritual understanding." In the Ephesians 1 prayer, Paul prayed that the Believers would receive "the spirit of wisdom and revelation in the knowledge of Him." In the Colossians 1 prayer, Paul is desiring that the Believers would be filled with the exact and precise knowledge of the will of God for their life. There are some Believers who have a small knowing of what God has called them to do, while others have a general understanding of what the will of God is for their life. In praying this prayer, Paul wants the Believer to fully know what God has called them to do.

With this precise knowledge, Paul is praying that the Believer would have the accompanying wisdom necessary to apply the knowledge that they have received. Many Believers can know the will of God for their life but not understand how to operate in it. There are also Believers who may know what God has called them to do but miss the timing of God to complete specifics of His will. These are just a few reasons why the Apostle would pray that the Believers would have this knowledge with "all wisdom and spiritual understanding." The word for understanding in the Greek is also defined as "a flowing together." Paul's use of this word gives the Believer a picture of two rivers; the two different rivers are a river of the precise knowledge of God's will and a river of wisdom and application. Paul is praying that these two rivers merge together producing an understanding in the Believer's spirit so they can live according to God's plan.

Walk Worthy of the Lord

"That ye might walk worthy of the Lord unto all pleasing, being fruitful in every good work, and increasing in the knowledge of God"

Col 1:10

As a result of the merging of the two rivers, the Believers would be able to "walk worthy of the Lord unto all pleasing, being fruitful in every good work, and increasing in the knowledge of God." When the Scriptures refer to walking in this sense, it is referring to a person regulating their life in a certain way so that they may make progress in that way. The merging of the rivers of the knowledge of the will of God with the river of correct application, enables the Believer to progress in a lifestyle that is suitable to what God has invited them to do. A Believer living this way is a living in a way that pleases God.

Being Fruitful in Every Good Work

This suitable lifestyle that is pleasing to God, is one that is fruitful in every good work. There are many good works that any given Believer may be called upon to do, but because of the merging of the rivers, a Believer will know the good works God has called for them to complete. In completing these good works, Believers will be fruitful in every work; every work will produce. This type of Believer is described in Psalm 1:3.

"And he shall be like a tree planted by the rivers of water, that bringeth forth his fruit in his season; his leaf also shall not wither; and whatsoever he doeth shall prosper."

Psalm 1:3

The Believer that allows the Spirit to produce the results of the Colossians prayer in their life, will prosper in whatever they do. God is very interested in a Believer's time, energy, talent, and treasure in producing at the highest level. God does not call people to do random assignments with no expectation of production. If God has invited the Believer to that assignment, God expects fruit and production. Jesus showed the Father's expectation of production in John 15.

"I am the true vine, and my Father is the husbandman. Every branch in me that beareth not fruit he taketh away: and every branch that beareth fruit, he purgeth it, that it may bring forth more fruit.

Now ye are clean through the word which I have spoken unto you. Abide in me, and I in you. As the branch cannot bear fruit of itself, except it abide in the vine; no more can ye, except ye abide in me. I am the vine, ye are the branches: He that abideth in me, and I in him, the same bringeth forth much fruit: for without me ye can do nothing. If a man abide not in me, he is cast forth as a branch, and is withered; and men gather them, and cast them into the fire, and they are burned."

John 15:1-6

In this teaching of Jesus, the Believer is shown how the Father increases production among those He has called. In the phrase "taketh away," Jesus is not saying that the Father throws away those who do not bear fruit. "Taketh away" refers to a gardening tactic, where the gardener lifts the non-producing vine closer to the sun and pairs it with a vine that is producing. God does not throw people away who are not producing, instead He lifts them out of the dust, brings them closer to Himself, and connects them with other Believers who are producing.

In this teaching, Jesus shares that all of those who bear fruit, the Father purges so that they can bring forth more fruit. God does not purge His people with sin, sickness, disease, disaster, harm, or any tool of the darkness. Jesus defines how the Father purges in verse three. The same word for "clean" is the same word that was translated as "purgeth" in verse two.   God purges His people through His Word. When a person reads the Word or listens to anointed teaching of the Word, God works on the Believer's heart about that Word; The Believer, recognizing God's voice, decides to adjust their thinking and align with that Word; then the Believer acts on the Word allowing the purging process to be completed and helps the Believer to produce more fruit.

Jesus continues in John 15, sharing that in order to bear fruit, the disciple must remain connected to Him.   The Believer cannot produce for God living apart from God. The Believer must maintain and increase their relationship with the Lord and remain in communication with Him.   Jesus made it very clear, that apart from Him a person can do nothing.   If a person tries to do things without Jesus, eventually, it will all turn into nothing.   A Believer that remembers that God lives in them and lives in close relationship with God, will be a very productive and fruitful citizen of God's kingdom.   Believers who do not live close lives with God, disconnect themselves and become withered. God does not want any Believer to be withered and resemble the world. God will not cut the Believer off from the life that flows from the vine, yet the Believer can choose to live a lifestyle that keeps them from experiencing the life that flows from the vine.   Yet, due to God's amazing mercy, the Believer can choose to repent and connect themselves to the vine again and be restored to life and productivity.

Always Increasing in the Knowledge of God

The suitable lifestyle that is pleasing to God is one that is always increasing in the knowledge of God. Once again, the Apostle is praying that Believer would increase in their intimate knowing of God. A Believer can live one thousand years and can still increase in their intimate knowing of God. This is meant to be a continual knowing and an everlasting process of discovery. As a Believer continues to increase in their knowledge of God, they do not come to a place where God is common to them. The Believer increasing in intimately knowing God, continues to grow to places on increasing awe, love, and adoration for their wonder-working God.

Strengthened with All Might

Strengthened with all might, according to his glorious power, unto all patience and longsuffering with joyfulness;

Col 1:11

In addition to the rivers merging and the Believer living a suitable lifestyle, Paul prays that the Believer would be "strengthened with all might, according to His glorious power." This prayer for strengthening is very similar to how Paul prayed in Ephesians chapter 3. The Believer who seeks to live a suitable life and fulfill the will of God for the life will need the strength of God. The Believer cannot complete their course with their own physical power and mental determination. In order for a Believer to be successful in this life, they must add to their own natural ability, the strength of the Almighty God. Being strengthened with God's glorious power enables the Believer to live with "all patience and longsuffering with joyfulness."

In praying this way, Paul is praying that the Believer have every type of patience and endurance that they need. With both words of patience and long-suffering pointing towards endurance and perseverance, the Believer is not supposed to be a wishy-washy person that is easily moved from their course or purpose. Paul is praying that these Believers live suitable lives that fulfill the call of God on their lives. In living a full life fulfilling the call of God, the Believer will run into challenges that will make them want to quit, give-up, or depart the path God has called them to follow. In praying this prayer, Paul is praying that Believers will develop a never quit attitude. The Apostle is praying that Believers would be constant in their pursuit of what God has called them to do. The use of both words should give Believers the encouragement that they should have "double patience." The patient endurance is not only for persevering through the challenges of life, but it is also for patiently enduring with other people. In order for the Believer to live the more excellent way of love, they must be patient with others. With "double patience," the Believer should live a suitable life that develops a "never quit" attitude while loving others through being patience with them.

The "double patience" suitable life is not a life that merely pushes through challenges to victory. It is a life that pushes through any challenge while being filled with joy. Joy is not an emotion or a feeling. As Galatians 5:22 reveals, joy is a fruit of the Spirit. When the Believer was born again, the Holy Spirit deposited joy in their heart. Nehemiah 8:10 shows that this joy is a source of strength. The Believer will be able to endure because they maintain their joy. Despite the worst storms, the Believer can have joy because they know that God is on their side and He always causes them to triumph. The Apostle Paul had this never quit joy-filled attitude.

But none of these things move me, neither count I my life dear unto myself, so that I might finish my course with joy, and the ministry, which I have received of the Lord Jesus, to testify the gospel of the grace of God.

Acts 20:24

As the Apostle referenced the hardships that were ahead of him, he said that none of those hardships moved him. He looked at His challenges and declared his outcome in advance, "I will finish my course with joy." By declaring this, Paul was stating that he would be victorious and he would not lose his joy in the process. The Apostle Paul is praying that Believers adopt this same attitude, because it is this attitude that leads to constant and consistent victory.

Giving Thanks

> *Giving thanks unto the Father, which hath made us meet to be partakers of the inheritance of the saints in light: Who hath delivered us from the power of darkness, and hath translated us into the kingdom of his dear Son: In whom we have redemption through his blood, even the forgiveness of sins:*
>
> *Col 1:12-14*

The Apostle concludes his prayer for the Believers in Colosse by thanking God for what He has done for every single Believer. Paul begins by thanking God giving all Believers the ability to access their inheritance of the abundance of glory. He continues His thanksgiving by declaring that God has delivered the Believer from the power of darkness. The word for "power" here is defined as authority. Notice, the tense the Apostle uses. The Believer has already been delivered from the authority of darkness. Satan cannot make the Believer do anything; he does not have the ability nor the authority. The Believer, through having their eyes covered in darkness, can decide to yield to Satan's plan, but Satan can never force the Believer to do anything. Anytime you hear a Believer say "The devil made me do it", you can rest assured they are mistaken. The devil may have deceived them, but they made the decision to act in disobedience to God's word.

When God delivered the Believer from the authority of darkness, He placed them into another kingdom. Every person is born into the kingdom of darkness under its authority, but when a person is born again, they are born into the kingdom of light. Paul calls the kingdom of light, the kingdom of God's "dear son." "Dear son" can also be translated as the Son of His Love. This kingdom of light is founded upon and filled with God's amazing love.

The Apostle continues by sharing that Believers have been rescued by the Blood of Jesus and have been granted the forgiveness of sin. Forgiveness, at its root, is a financial term. It refers to the cancelling of debt. When God cancelled the Believer's sin, He cancelled their sin debt . This phrase should remind the Believer, as Ephesians 2:8 teaches, salvation is a gift. It is not a thing that can be achieved by enough good works. If salvation could be achieved through works, it would be a wage and not a gift. Salvation is a gift. Through the Blood of Jesus, God cancelled every debt caused by sin. It is a well-meaning religious notion for Believers to say that they owe God for all He has done for them. Although it is well-meaning, and sounds good, it is doctrinally incorrect. Because of the Blood of Jesus and the forgiveness of sins, the Believer does not owe God anything. He cancelled their debt. It because of this great act of love, the Believer decides to dedicate their life to God, His will, and His commands. It is not a decision based on debt, but one out of extreme gratitude. If a Believer keeps this mindset, they will be more gracious in their dealings with others. This grateful mindset will enable the Believer to be more patient with others because the Believer understands all God has done for them..

In conclusion, the Colossians 1 prayer is a prayer that enables Believers to live a suitable life before God that is filled with the knowledge of God's will, all spiritual understanding, strength, patience, joy, and gratefulness for what God has done.

Before continuing to the bonus chapter, take a few moments and pray this prayer for yourself:

Father,

I pray that You will fill me with the knowledge of Your will in all wisdom and spiritual understanding; so that I might walk worthy of you, Lord, unto all pleasing, being fruitful in every good work, and increasing in the knowledge of You, strengthened with all might, according to Your glorious power, unto all patience and long-suffering with joyfulness. Father, I give you thanks for enabling me to be a partaker of the inheritance of the saints in light: You have delivered me from the power of darkness, and have translated me into the kingdom of Your dear Son: In Jesus I have redemption through His blood and the forgiveness of sins. I thank you for these things in Jesus' Name, Amen.

BONUS: THE 2ND THESSALONIANS 3 PRAYER

PRAYER FOR SPIRITUAL LEADERS

Every Believer needs a Pastor and every Believer needs to belong to a church family. Most Believers have the correct understanding that their Pastor should be a person of prayer. Even though a Pastor should be a person of prayer, it is the responsibility of the congregation to pray for their spiritual leader continually. There are different instances in Scripture where Paul requests prayer for himself. The prayer in 2nd Thessalonians chapter 3 is one of those instances. This is a prayer that every Believer should continually pray for their spiritual leader and for the men and women of God that speak into their lives.

The Word Will Have Free Course

Finally, brethren, pray for us, that the word of the Lord may have free course, and be glorified, even as it is with you: 2 And that we may be delivered from unreasonable and wicked men: for all men have not faith.

2nd Thessalonians 3:1-2

The Apostle asks that the church pray that "the word of the Lord may have free course." In speaking of the "word of the Lord," Paul is referring to the message that God has instructed his team to minister. In praying that the Word has "free course," the church would be praying that the message Paul and his team preaches overcomes everything that tries to hinder or stop it. This prayer for "free course" is also a prayer that asks for the Word to multiply quickly. The Word of God increasing and multiplying quickly is a time where the message that is preached rapidly spreads among the population in the surrounding area that it is preached in. This is not a normal spread of information, but a supernatural rate of expansion that effects the entire region. As seen in the Book of Acts, when the Word spreads this way, many people hear, believe, and obey the Gospel of the Lord Jesus Christ.

Pray for the Message to be Glorified

In addition to this supernatural propagation of the message of Christ, Paul wants the church to pray for the message to be "glorified." A message that is "glorified," is held in high esteem, celebrated, and honored. Paul adds a phrase at the end of verse one that indicates the Word is glorified among the Thessalonians. In studying the time frame and the messages of 1st and 2nd Thessalonians, it is portrayed that the churches of Thessalonica experienced rapid and sustainable spiritual growth. Paul desires for

Corinth, the city where Paul was writing from, to experience the same type of spiritual growth that the Thessalonians had experienced and to honor the Word just as the Thessalonians had honored the Word.

Paul closes his request for prayer, with a request for protection and deliverance. The Apostle asks the church pray that he and his team are "delivered from wicked and unreasonable men." "Wicked and unreasonable men" were not just people who did not believe Paul's message, but they were individuals who set themselves to oppose and stop the spread of the message Paul was preaching. These individuals were plotting harm and evil things for the message and its messengers. As a result of their tactics and plots, Paul requested for prayer that they would be rescued from all of their attempts to stop their ministry.

Through the work of the Holy Spirit, the efforts of Paul and his team, and the effective prayers of those in Thessalonica, a thriving church was founded in Corinth. The city of Corinth was known for its extreme immorality. Yet because of the prayers of the Believers and the power of the Holy Spirit, the apostolic team was successful in their mission. Every Believer should pray for their Pastor the way the Thessalonians prayed for the Apostle Paul.

Before finishing this book, take a few moments and pray this prayer for your Pastor, your spiritual leaders, and those who spiritually speak into your life:

Father,
I pray for my Pastor, my spiritual leaders, and those who spiritually speak and pour into my life. I pray the messages that you give them, the word of the Lord, may have free course and be glorified. I pray that you will deliver them from unreasonable and wicked men: for all men have not faith. Father, I thank you for my Pastor, my spiritual leaders, those who spiritually speak into my life, and for what you are doing in their lives. In Jesus' name I pray, Amen.

ABOUT THE AUTHOR

Kerrick A. R. Butler II is a graduate of Word of Faith Bible Training Center (Class of 2005) and of Oral Roberts University (Class of 2009). Kerrick serves as Senior Pastor of Faith Christian Center in Austell, Ga. Kerrick, and his wife Racquel, believe wholeheartedly in sharing the message of Jesus through creative avenues which help the reader easily apply the message to their everyday life. Kerrick, Racquel, and their beautiful daughters reside in the Metro Atlanta area.

OTHER PUBLICATIONS BY THE AUTHOR

BIBLICAL HEROES VOLUME ONE

Released: January 2015

Imagine. What if you could sit down with five Biblical Heroes for an hour, what would you ask them and what would they tell you? Prepare for a journey into the supernatural as you find out in Biblical Heroes Volume One!

CONFESSIONS FOR THE HEART

Released: October 2015

In life, there are times so challenging that we just focus on getting to the other side. With all of our strength, we push through the pain, weather the storm, overcome obstacles, and fight the good fight until we have won. After the battle, when the storm has ceased, how often do we do a checkup on our heart? In this brief eBook, learn one of the ways to help your heart recover from the hardships of life and how to strengthen it to help you conquer any challenge in life.

CONFESSIONS FOR THE MIND

Released: November 2015

When it comes to the Word of God, many people only focus on the aspects that relate to the spirit or the heart of a person. If attention is only given to the spirit of a person, that individual will miss out on many of the great benefits God has for them in this life. Confessions For The Mind focuses on an aspect of the human soul. It looks at what the Bible has to say concerning the mind, understanding, thought process, imagination, creativity and how to unlock the potential that God has made available to every believer.

FAITH AND LOVE: A DAILY DEVOTIONAL

Released: October 2016

This 31-day devotional is designed to inspire and strengthen your faith. As a believer, faith and love are two of the most important topics in the Word of God that affect your everyday life. These two powerful spiritual forces are connected and if you allow them to consistently work in your life, nothing will be impossible for you.

THE LIBRARIAN

Released: December 2016

At some point in every person's life, they wonder, "Why I am here? What is my purpose?" In the Librarian, Kerrick helps the reader answer those important questions. Through this parable and the subsequent chapters, you will be inspired and challenged to discover and live your God-given purpose.

Made in the USA
Lexington, KY
30 September 2019